ALL ABOUT FLORIDA

100+ Amazing & Interesting Facts & Trivia

By Bandana Ojha

Introduction

Filled with up-to-date information, fascinating & fun facts this book " All About Florida: 100+ Amazing & Interesting Facts with Pictures" is the best book for kids to find out more about the Sunshine State. This book would satisfy the children's curiosity and help them to understand why Florida is special—and what makes it different from other States. This book gives a story, history, the state symbols, how FL got her name, why it is called Sunshine State, why FL attracts millions of visitors every year & explores the most interesting and amazing fun facts about Florida. It is a fun and fascinating way for young readers to find out more interesting and fun facts of Florida. This is a great chance for every kid to expand their knowledge about the Alligator state and impress family and friends with all "discovered and never knew before" amazing fun facts.

1. On March 3, 1845, Florida was annexed to the United States of America, becoming the 27th U.S. state.

2. Florida is the southernmost contiguous state in the United States.

3. It is the 22nd largest and 3rd most populous state in the nation

4. Florida was the first region of the continental United States to be visited and settled by Europeans.

5. When Juan Ponce de León reached Florida, it was already inhabited by Native American tribes, just like most other places on the continent. Some of the tribes who lived here before the Europeans came were the Apalachee, Calusa, Creek, Ais, and Timucua.

6. Saint Augustine is the oldest European settlement in North America.

7. Florida is bordered to the west by the Gulf of Mexico, to the northwest by Alabama, to the north by Georgia, to the east by the Atlantic Ocean, and to the south by the Straits of Florida.

8. The population of Florida was about 21.48 million in 2019.

9. Florida boasts 1,300 miles of coastline and 800 miles of beaches.

10. The State Abbreviation of Florida is "FL".

11. The State follows EST (Eastern Standard Time).

12. People who live in Florida or who come from Florida are called Floridians.

13. Florida was named by Ponce de Leon a Spanish Explorer in 1512. "la Florida," he called this land, Spanish for flowery or covered with flowers.

14. The flag of Florida is the state flag of the U.S. state of Florida. It consists of a red saltire on a white background, with the state seal superimposed on the center.

15. The flag was first adopted as the state flag of Florida in 1868.
16. The flag's current design has been in use since May 21, 1985, after the Florida state seal was graphically altered and officially sanctioned for use by state officials.

17. The Great Seal of the State of Florida is used to represent the government of the state of Florida.

18. The State Seal is commonly used on state government buildings, vehicles, and other effects of the state government. It also appears on the state flag of Florida.

19. The University of Florida was granted the honor of using the seal as its university seal.

20. The State nick name is "The Sunshine State".

21. The name "Sunshine State" comes from the high amounts of sunshine the state receives every year. On average Florida receives about 2927 hours of sunshine per year and temperatures can reach into the 100s on a given summers day.

22. The State Capital is Tallahassee.

23. The State Motto is "In God We Trust".

24. The state flower of Florida is Orange blossom.

25. The state wildflower is Tickseed.

26. The state fruit is Orange.

27. The state tree is Sabal palm.

28. The state animal is Florida panther

29. The state bird is Northern mockingbird.

30. The state butterfly is Zebra longwing.

31. The state fish is largemouth bass.

32. The state saltwater fish is Atlantic sailfish.

33. The state heritage cattle breed is Florida Cracker cattle.

34. The state horse is Florida Cracker Horse.

35. The state mammal (marine) is Florida manatee.

36. The state mammal (salt water) is Porpoise.

37. The state Reptile is American alligator.

38. The state Reptile (salt water) is Loggerhead sea turtle.

39. The state shell is Horse conch.

40. The state tortoise is Gopher tortoise.

41. The state beverage is Orange juice.

42. The state Pie is Key lime pie.

43. The state play is Cross and Sword.

44. The state soil is Myakka soil.

45. The state stone is Agatized coral.

46. The state Rodeo is Silver Spurs Rodeo.

47. The state Gem is Moonstone.

48. Everglades National Park in Florida is the only place in the world which is home to both the American crocodile and the American alligator.

49. Gatorade was named for the University of Florida Gators where the drink was first developed.

50. Florida has more toll roads, bridges, and golf courses than any other state in the nation.

51. Florida is the only state that has 2 rivers both with the same name. There is a Withlacoochee in north central Florida and a Withlacoochee in central Florida. They have nothing in common except the name.

52. Florida has more than 26,000 square miles of forests, covering about half of the state's land area.

53. The largest metropolitan area in the state as well as the entire southeastern United States is the Miami metropolitan area, with about 6.06 million people.

54. Fort Lauderdale is nicknamed Venice of America because it has an extensive network of canals,165 miles of waterways within the city limits.

55. Florida produces 70% of the oranges in the United States and supplies 40% of the world's orange juice.

56. Florida is also the largest producer of watermelons, strawberries, sugar, and tomatoes.

57. Florida is the second largest producer of Grapefruit in whole world. The first position is captured by Brazil.

58. Florida is the second-largest producer of tomatoes in whole of USA. Both California and Florida grow tomatoes of 30,000 to 40,000 acres of land every year. That is 2/3rd of total tomato acreage in whole nation.

59. Greater Miami is the only metropolitan area in America with two national parks: Everglades National Park and Biscayne National Park.

60. Florida is the world's top travel destination with 90 million visitors every year.

61. Walt Disney World Resort is the planet's most visited and biggest recreational resort.

62. Almost 50 million people visit the Walt Disney World Resort on an annual basis.

63. Magic Kingdom is the 3rd most popular tourist attraction in the world.

64. Over 7% of Florida's total area is water.

65. Central Florida is known as the lightning capital of the United States because the region experiences more lightning strikes than anywhere else in the country.

66. Lake Okeechobee is the largest freshwater lake in Florida. It is the third largest freshwater lake in the United States.

67. Jacksonville, Florida is the largest city in the conterminous United States.

68. Dick Pope, the founder of Cypress Gardens, is known as the "Father of Florida Tourism".

69. Mechanical refrigeration was invented in Florida in 1851 by Dr. John Gorrie.

70. Florida is the space capital of the United States.

71. In 1958, the first U.S. satellite Explorer I was launched from Cape Canaveral.

72. NASA's first communication satellite "Echo 1" was launched from Cape Canaveral, Florida on August 12, 1960.

73. Florida is also known for the establishment of the first commercial space launching industry in the United States.

74. Neil Armstrong, the first man to walk on the moon was launched from the Kennedy Space Centre in Florida on July 16, 1969.

75. Castillo de San Marcos in St. Augustine, Florida is the oldest masonry fort in the United States.

76. The Wakulla Springs in Tallahassee, Florida is the world's largest and deepest freshwater spring.

77. Florida is the U.S. state with most first magnitude springs.

78. Key Largo, on the Florida Keys is known as the Dive Capital of the World.

79. The first suntan lotion was invented by Miami Beach pharmacist, Benjamin Green in 1944.

80. Benjamin Green invented it by cooking cocoa butter in a granite pot. He used his wife's stove to do so.

81. Disney World decorates more than 1,500 Christmas trees at holiday time.

82. According to state law every building used for public purposes must have outward opening doors due to the strong winds which occur during hurricane.

83. Florida's oldest tree is 3500 years old and is still standing strong. It is a Cypress tree called the "Senator" and is located just north of Longwood at Big Tree Park of Florida.

84. Key West has the highest recorded average temperature in the United States.

85. Tampa's Bayshore Boulevard is publicized as the world's longest continuous sidewalk. It is a popular waterfront gathering place for joggers and in-line skaters.

86. The Bailey-Matthews National Shell Museum in the city of Sanibel is the only museum in the world that is dedicated entirely to the study of shells and mollusks.

87. Florida is the flattest state in the U.S. followed by Illinois, North Dakota, Louisiana, Minnesota, Delaware, and Kansas.

88. Florida has the highest percentage of people over 65 of age.

89. Florida also holds the record of having the shortest donkey in the world. Born in October 2007, KneeHi is the shortest donkey measuring at 64.2 cm.

90. There are no dinosaur fossils in Florida.

91. Florida is the flattest state in America.

92. The highest temperature recorded in Florida is 109°, Fahrenheit. This record high was recorded on June 29, 1931 at Monticello.

93. The lowest temperature in Florida, -2°, was recorded on February 13, 1899 at Tallahassee, the state capital.

94. The highest point in Florida is Britton Hill, Lakewood Park in Walton County and is only 345 feet above sea level.

95. The lowest point in Florida is sea level where Florida meets the Atlantic Ocean and the Gulf of Mexico.

96. The small town of Pierson in Northeast Florida is known as the Fern Capital of the World.

97. Florida's largest river, the St. Johns River, is one of only a few major rivers that flow from south to north.

98. The Belleview Biltmore Resort and Spa, northwest of Tampa Bay is said to be the world's largest occupied wooden structure at 820,000 square feet.

99. The world's first scheduled commercial airline flight from St. Petersburg, FL to Tampa, FL took place on January 1, 1914 and was completed by a young pilot named Tony Jannus.

100. Florida was the site of largest battle fought during the American Civil War. The battle is commemorated by the Olustee Battlefield State Historic Site.

101. Islamorada in Florida is known as the Sports Fishing Capital of the World.

102. The only museum in whole of the United States of America that is dedicated to Japan's living culture is in Florida. It is the Morikami Museum located at Delray Beach.

103. Fellsmere – a small town in Florida is known for hosting the annual Frog Leg Festival. The town has entered the Guinness World Record for hosting the largest Frog Leg Festival.

Please check this out:

Our other best-selling books for kids are-

Know about **Sharks**: 100 Amazing Fun Facts with Pictures

Know About **Whales**:100+ Amazing & Interesting Fun Facts with Pictures: " Never known Before "- Whales facts

Know About **Dinosaurs**: 100 Amazing & Interesting Fun Facts with Pictures

Know About **Kangaroos**: Amazing & Interesting Facts with Pictures

Know About **Penguins**: 100+ Amazing Penguin Facts with Pictures

Know About **Dolphins** :100 Amazing Dolphin Facts with Pictures

Know About **Elephant** :100 Amazing Dolphin Facts with Pictures

All About **New York**: 100+ Amazing Facts with Pictures

All About **New Jersey**: 100+ Amazing Facts with Pictures

All About **Massachusetts**: 100+ Amazing Facts with Pictures

All About **Florida**: 100+ Amazing Facts with Pictures

All About **California**: 100+ Amazing Facts with Pictures

All About **Arizona**: 100+ Amazing Facts with Pictures

All About **Texas**: 100+ Amazing Facts with Pictures
All About **Minnesota**: 100+ Amazing Facts with Pictures
All About **Italy**: 100+ Amazing Facts with Pictures
All About **France**: 100+ Amazing Facts with Pictures
All About **Japan:** 100 Amazing & Interesting Fun Facts
100 Amazing **Quiz Q & A About Penguin**: Never Known Before Penguin Facts Most Popular **Animal Quiz** book for Kids: 100 amazing animal facts
Quiz Book for Kids: Science, History, Geography, Biology, Computer & Information Technology
English **Grammar** for Kids: Most Easy Way to learn English Grammar
Solar System & Space Science- Quiz for Kids: What You Know About Solar System English
Grammar Practice Book for elementary kids: 1000+ Practice Questions with Answers
A to Z of **English Tense**
My First **Fruits**

43

Made in United States
Orlando, FL
26 March 2022